The Gifted Introvert: Your Hidden Tools For Success

A Seven Step Programme To Help You Achieve

By Mary Jane Boholst and Richard Daniel Curtis

First edition published 3/18

ISBN 13: 978-1-912010-10-3

Ebook ISBN 13: 978-1-912010-11-0

Published by: TKC Ltd

For more details on Richard's work, please go to

www.richarddanielcurtis.com

For more details on Mary Jane's work, please go to

www.conscious-cocoon.co.uk

The Gifted Introvert:

Your Hidden Tools For Success

Contents

About The Authors 167

Introduction

Welcome to this programme and thank you for picking it up!

We are guessing that you are here because you identify yourself as an introvert or have features of introversion that you'd like to change or learn how to utilise for success. It may be that you'd like to cope better in social situations, or you'd like to find ways of talking to people you don't know. Maybe you'd like to be more confident at work or you'd like to be able to tell your family how to help you. Whatever it is, we feel the seven steps contained in this programme (a gift from us to you) will help you think about your introversion differently and move you forward on your journey.

Having an introvert personality type is not an illness, a disability or anything that should hold you back. The causes were shown in the 1980s to be 39-58% genetic, combined with a number of other environmental factors (family only playing a small part). Being an introvert can be a huge blessing. Yes, there are disadvantages, but actually as two introverts running successful businesses both of us can attest to the great benefits.

Traditionally introverts are seen as quiet, reflective and like to be alone rather than social. Common perception tells us that introverts need to withdraw into their shells after social gatherings. However, there has been recent research into introversion, showing that no one behaves as an introvert or an extrovert all of the time, that even extroverts can be exhausted from socialising and need to recoup with some 'me' time. Another misconception around introversion is in the field of sales. Traditionally sales people have been thought of as extrovert and for introverts it was seen as a role not suited to them. However, research now shows that extroverts and introverts perform about the same, but the most successful people are a mixture of both (known as 'ambiverts').

Throughout this programme, we do not seek to make you an extrovert. We want you to see the gift that you have inside you and encourage you to embrace that gift, whilst overcoming the parts that are holding you back.

Richard grew up in Southampton, on the south coast of the UK. By the time he was in secondary school, Richard's disability (severe eczema affecting the use of his hands) and self-image led to him being bullied enormously. Richard learnt that it was best to keep himself to himself, be the outsider and to be a wall flower in public situations.

Fast forward 20 years, Richard is a multi-award-winning business owner, a leading behaviour expert, an internationally renowned author and has been on most of the UK television channels. He still lives in Southampton with his girlfriend and their baby son, training others about psychology and mentoring through his business The Mentoring School and studying part-time for a PhD in Psychology. He's still an introvert and would much rather than stand and watch the crowds than host the conferences he runs, but as he puts it "the way I cope with my introversion is by being extrovert around others."

Mary Jane grew up in South West London. Her parents worked two jobs each to keep a roof over their heads and food on the table. At three months old she developed eczema on her face that over her childhood years made her feel ashamed and different. By the time she reached secondary school she was known for not participating in class and not standing out of the crowd.

Currently she is a successful speaker and coach helping introverted entrepreneurs to grow their businesses. Speaking at events at Google Campus, the City Business Library and the Geek Girl Conference. She still lives in London and is still very much an introvert, but has shed the shyness that held her back by confronting her fears of public speaking, networking and creating a successful business.

We met each other through a conference on Mental Health that Richard was chairing. Instantly recognising the connection and the power of each other's stories, we vowed to do something to support introverts to see the benefits and the power they hold.

In this programme, we will share with you the stages that we both went through to get to where we are now. That doesn't mean that we recognised them as steps, no one had designed a blueprint or trail for us for follow, they were just things that we had both done to become more self-aware of our gifts. That's part of the reason we wrote this programme, to let others see the steps we both felt were vital to our own self-discovery journeys.

We lay out the seven steps to understanding yourself and the things that make you tick. We'll take you through a journey, beginning with Step 1 Recognising Success. In this Step, you'll learn about setting yourself goals, recognising that you are moving towards them and most importantly how to use failure as a way of moving you forward.

Step 2 is all about looking inside you and learning to accept all of you, even the soft squidgy bits or the little self-loathing voice in your head.

Step 3 takes you through a self-assessment of your support networks and how to use them in your journey to success.

This is followed by a look at how the world sees you in Step 4, helping you to deal with any misconceptions you feel others have about you.

In Step 5 we look at how to communicate your personality to others, how to deal with your emotions and stop the emotions of other people having a huge impact on you.

Step 6 is all about peak performance, dealing with doubt and how to succeed.

And finally, in Step 7, we discuss contentment and fulfilment and how to recognise them.

Throughout the lessons, we will ask you to carry out a reflective task to help you to move towards your goals. We recommend buying a special journal especially to record your journey, to do the activities and record your progress. Once you have completed the programme, take the time to flick back through and reflect on the journey you have made.

Please read this programme once through, working through the activities in each lesson. As you do these they will help you to identify the key learning. Many people choose to go through this programme two, three or more times – each time adding a layer of awareness and confidence in dealing with the issues worrying them. No matter how many times you read this, we know that you will benefit from it.

Now, grab a new journal, a pen and an open mind…

We give you the gift within you…

We give you The Gifted Introvert…

Step 1 - Recognising Success

Activity 1

In your journal, write on a page what the biggest social problem you feel you face is.

How does it make you feel?

Lesson 1 - How To Set Goals

Setting goals is the first step to turning the invisible into the visible

Tony Robbins

Many people talk about the importance of goal setting, but far less will talk to you about the process of how to set goals. Many will want to push you out of your comfort zone and force you to take action, but we say take heed of the contents of this lesson if you do.

The psychology of our comfort zone is an interesting one, and involves a major theory – the hedonic treadmill effect and is the reason money doesn't make us happy on its own, amongst many other things. Going back to the 1970s it was called the hedonic adaptation effect and was used to describe how, as one becomes more used to new events in life (a study in 1978 looked at lottery winners), that their emotions normalise at that level and so their concept of how happy they feel remains the same – money doesn't buy you happiness, as you become richer, the things you worry about change (for example whether people will try and take your money) and so your happiness level remains the same as it was before. This level isn't necessarily neutral and can change over time.

The theory was updated to become the hedonic treadmill theory in the 1990s and research has continued into the effect since then. Some suggest that we are predisposed to have a certain happiness/stress level, others that it is affected by events in our lives (more so negative events). Either way, the risk is that you move yourself to a new situation (e.g. divorce, get a new job, achieve a milestone) and unless we do something to change our happiness level longer-term, then it will return to where it was.

How is this relevant to goal setting? Because just setting a goal and achieving it will not bring around long-term change in your happiness level. As you acclimatise to the new level you find yourself in, then you are likely to end up mentally returning to where you are already without something else kicking in. That's part of the reason we have designed this programme like we have, it's alright getting you to set goals, but just achieving them isn't enough, we need to help you to recognise how to make other changes in your life.

The other thing we want to warn you about goal setting is the amount of stress you put yourself under. Now, this isn't an excuse to not put yourself outside of your comfort zone and stay where you are, this is a word of warning about what happens if you go too far. There are several theories out there that say when you are within your 'comfort zone' you don't make progress, because you are comfortable where you are. If you then move yourself too far outside of your comfort zone, then the amount of stress you experience can also paralyse you. The bit in-between the two can sometimes be referred to as the 'optimal performance zone' or the area you want to push yourself into so that you experience some drive, anxiety and stress to force you to take action, but not too much, so that it overwhelms you:

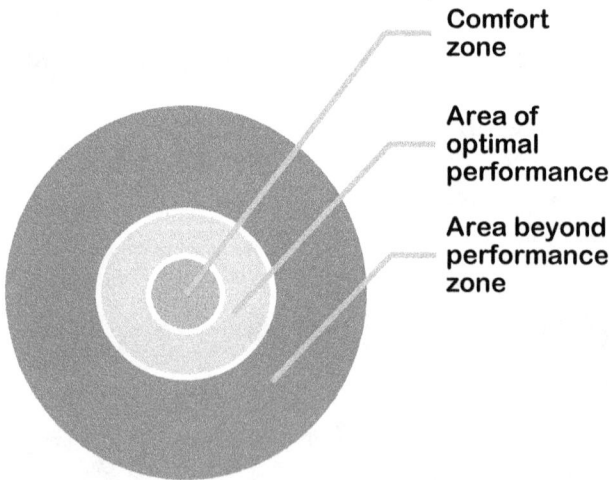

Comfort zone

Area of optimal performance

Area beyond performance zone

All-in-all goal setting is a tricky beast. Some people say to have a huge goal of a lifetime, whereas others see that as too far away and unobtainable. The reality is that if you want to achieve a hugely significant goal, then along the way you need to break it down into smaller goals that are not too easy to achieve, but are on the horizon, so you can see it, desire it and force yourself to move towards it.

Let us tell you about something else relevant about what's happening in your body – the hormone system. When you are working towards something, for example pushing yourself to reach a goal, a good hormone called dopamine gets released. This is like a searching drug and pushes you to keep going until you have achieved. At that point, endorphins take over, make you feel amazing (and also take away some of the pain you may be feeling at that point) and in an ideal world counteract the dopamine build-up. To go back several millennia, dopamine kept you going whilst you searched for food for long hours, you keep searching throughout the night and eventually success – you find food, enough for a week and feel on top of the world!

Well, that's how it should work. Unfortunately, there are several things that can interrupt that. Have you ever checked your phone, the light's not blinking, so therefore swiped the screen – still no message? But to be sure, you then open your social media or email and hit refresh – nothing? You have barely put it down before you start that cycle again. This is called a dopamine loop, the dopamine is keeping you searching and even when you do get a message, it just is not enough to satisfy you, so you reply straight away or check to see if someone else has messaged you. To put it simply, the reward you are getting is not enough to overcome the amount of dopamine in your system.

The solution? To stop and force your dopamine level to reduce. By forcing yourself each day to have time away from the technology keeping your dopamine levels raised, you force your brain to reduce the levels needed. It's a very healthy practice to get yourself into. This theory, combined with the hedonic treadmill effect described above, are the reason that for many it takes us a few days to relax on holiday - our body needs to normalise the stress and dopamine levels.

And the same is true of goals without rewards. If you move from one goal to the next, to the next, without stopping to feel that endorphin rush, then you are constantly relying on dopamine to keep you going. Over time, you will find it harder to feel that sense of achievement and your body will get used to being in a perpetual dopamine loop.

Our advice is to make sure that as you map out your goals (see below), then take the time to plan in your endorphin rushes – your rewards or treats – along the way, that way as you push yourself to move forward, then you know exactly what treat you have lined up for yourself. You might even plan bronze, silver and gold rewards, so that even if you didn't reach that goal when you planned to, or you just missed it, you give yourself a smaller reward to help with this cycle and give yourself a little endorphin rush.

When it comes to setting your goals, to begin with, think about where you are trying to get to in the end. Think about that huge great big massive goal, whether it be to speak in front of several hundred people, to post online videos, or to attend the party you want to go to. Imagine what it feels like, sounds like, and smells like.

But then, you need to take a mental step backwards – if that is the end of your journey, what was the step before it? What did you achieve at that stage? What does that look and feel like when you are stood there?

And the one before that? Keep tracking it back until you get to where you are now.

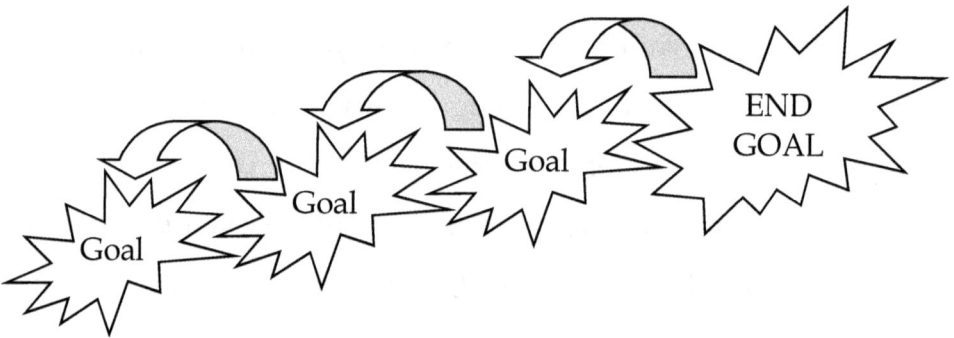

Congratulations, you have just set your goals on this journey to success!

Activity 2

What are you wanting to achieve by taking this programme?

Write your target in your journal.

What are your steps along the way?

What things will you notice along the way?

Lesson 2 - How To Celebrate Small Steps

I don't focus on what I'm up against. I focus on my goals and I try to ignore the rest.

Venus Williams

With your goals from the previous activity you are well on your way to success, and it's important to celebrate the small achievements to keep you moving forward.

The science shows that achieving targets releases the hormone dopamine, which feels good and encourages us to keep going toward our goals.

When we can break our large goal down into smaller steps that means that we get to enjoy the effect of taking action on a regular basis which just encourages us to keep going, and makes it so that before we know it we've reached our goal!

An easy way to know if you are moving toward or away from your goal is to look at your goal and give it a deadline, then work backward to see what the monthly, weekly, daily and perhaps even hourly targets should be.

When writing this programme Mary Jane and Richard set out the Steps and word count then we set a deadline for a draft to be done by. Mary Jane took her sections and deadline and on a weekly basis wrote a section at a time. She knew that if she wanted to get a section done a week that she had to write 1000 words a week, split over 5 days that was just 200 words a day!

When you break down your goal into smaller chunks or tasks you may need to figure out if the task is small enough to achieve easily or not.

One way of doing that is using a technique called muscle testing. This involves is using your body to figure out if something is right for you.

The idea is that you can use your body's inherent knowing to help you make decisions. You might think this is all a bit too weird, but have you ever had the experience of being somewhere or meeting someone where you just got a bad vibe and knew that it was bad for you? That's your intuition and your body's way of alerting you to and protecting you from danger.

It is something that you can tune into at any time without having to be in danger first!

How you do that is by using one of the following techniques. One is to make an 'O' shape using the thumb and a finger of one hand, then use the index finger of the other to see if you can break the circle.

Take note of how much force you need to break the circle each time you do this.

Bring to mind someone or something that you love and again try and break the circle.

Then bring to mind someone or something you feel less fondly for or about and break the circle, you'll notice a huge difference.

You can also take the middle finger of your non-dominant hand and place it above the index finger of the same hand and see how much pressure it takes to push down your index finger when you think of something positive and also something negative.

If you have a friend that you can ask you could also ask them to help you to do this (and maybe you could help them to do this too!) Stand with one or both arms out in front of you and hold them there. Ask your friend to try and push them down while you think of something positive and something negative.

What you may find is that when you think of something positive you stay strong and the circle doesn't break so easily, nor the finger or arm move as much than when you think of something negative.

Another way that also allows us to tap into our body's knowing is to stand up, take a few deep breaths, close your eyes and clear your mind. Then imagine the scenario or options we are confronted with, for example, stay in and study or go out with my friends, step to one side and imagine the first option. Notice how your body feels about it. Then step to the other side and imagine doing that, again noticing how you feel about it.

The option that feels the lightest and more expansive is the option that your body prefers.

Try these out and see which one/s work for you. Mary Jane prefers the more visceral exercise of standing and imagining the options. Richard likes to close his eyes and ask a yes or no question, if his body leans forward it is a yes and backwards is a no.

Whichever works for you, you can then use the technique you prefer to check if something will help you to move towards your goal. Simply bring to mind the action/option and use the technique to see which the right fit is for you!

Once you've identified the actions you need to take, it's important to make sure that you celebrate them, not just the big goals. In terms of this programme it could be completing any of the activities or reading just one more page, lesson or paragraph.

How you celebrate is up to you. You might like to have a reward for completing each lesson that then contributes to a bigger reward for reaching the end of the programme. Maybe you award yourself a gold star for each completed Step and when you have all 7 stars you award yourself something that you want; perhaps a music download or new game or book. If you share this journey with others, you could ask for contributions towards a concert ticket or a shopping trip.

On the journey to any goal you are likely to encounter resistance inside your mind. Resistance sounds like the voice in your head that says "I'm too tired I can't do it now", "I don't have the time to do this", "I don't have the energy", "When I do... then I'll do the next lesson", and even "I don't have enough knowledge to do this."

It's important to know that this is a normal and natural part of learning to do something new, and that it is something that can stop you from succeeding if you aren't aware of it.

What often happens when someone is not aware of resistance, they will hear the voice that says "I'm too tired" or "I can't be bothered" and it will mean that they stop and go and do something else instead and it takes them away from what they really wanted to achieve.

When you are aware of resistance you can hear the voice and actively choose to listen to it and follow what it says or listen and say "thank you for showing me I'm on the right path" and then continuing on with what you are doing.

The thing is that if you are learning to do something new and wanting to succeed at something it will feel uncomfortable and resistance will pop up because it is not what you are used to. Resistance is really just our brains way of keeping us safe from the unknown, we can allow it to stop us or we can use it as the sign post it really is and challenge ourselves to do something new!

Activity 3

Write in your journal the signs that make you know that you have made the right decision.

How does it feel?

What do you do?

What things do you say?

How do you know you are going in the right direction?

Lesson 3 - Seeing Failure As Feedback

It's fine to celebrate success but it is more important to heed the lessons of failure

Bill Gates

Failure is a necessary part of success. A lot of the technologies and inventions we use and take for granted today came about because someone kept going, despite failure, to make them a reality. Any successful business person, writer, actor, singer or celebrity has only succeeded because they have failed.

One example is Thomas Edison, the inventor of the light bulb, who took thousands of attempts to create the first working bulb. J.K Rowling the author of the hugely popular and successful Harry Potter series was a divorced single parent living on benefits before she had success with Harry Potter and became a millionaire!

The thing about failure is that it is often just showing us where we need to improve or make adjustments before we can achieve the success we are looking for.

It's when we can see the lessons in the failure that we can move forward toward our goal and success. Like when a teacher corrects our work and helps us to achieve the grades and marks that we desire.

Usually what stops us from reaching a goal is our fear of failure. Usually that's because we see failure as making a fool of ourselves. But if we shift from thinking of failure as a signal to stop, to a signal to pause and correct what isn't working, then it opens the pathway for us to learn from failure and allow us to keep growing and moving forward.

Often it is the fear of making a mistake and being seen as a failure that can stop us from moving forward.

Fear is really the false assumptions and expectations that we have about the outcome of a particular situation. They can feel like they are the truth and will definitely happen. However, usually when we confront the fear that we have we can find that it is just an illusion created by our mind to keep us safe.

Fear is a useful response to certain experiences that can spur us into the appropriate action like for example being chased by a lion or escaping a fire, and sometimes instead of spurring action, it can cause us to freeze instead.

When we become mindful and aware of the fact that fear is stopping us and what kind of fear we are experiencing (especially the fear of failure), we can use it to look at what we can do to mitigate or lessen the possible outcomes that we fear and get into action anyway.

We can look at what the worst case scenario might be and what if anything we can do to avoid that outcome.

If the reason you haven't applied for the job that you really want is because they might reject you, what can you do to avoid or lessen the effects of that outcome? Perhaps you make sure that you write the best CV and covering letter that you can. Perhaps you get some support to do that and maybe you also apply for other jobs or get to know someone who works in the company and ask them to put in a good word for you.

If you don't get the job how can you use that experience to keep you moving forward? Perhaps you ask for feedback and advice on what you could have done differently or you simply ask yourself what you could do differently next time.

The actress Lisa Kudrow actually got fired from one of her more high-profile roles before she was cast in Friends and made it big as an actor.

Richard was considered poor at behaviour management as a teacher, it was holding back his career. He quit and began to teach in a unit for children with severe behaviour problems to gain that experience. Due to an unfortunate incident resulting in the teacher-in-charge going off long-term sick, he quickly ended up in charge and that was the beginning of a now international reputation.

Mary Jane struggled to get clients in the early days of her business before she took steps to manage her introversion and fear of public speaking and begin to speak in public, which boosted her sales and her business.

It helps to remember that it's OK to not be perfect, no one is, but keep at it and don't give up because you never know you may find you invent the next best app or start up or write the next bestseller.

The only real failure is not just quitting or stopping, but not learning the lessons and if you stay committed and determined to reach your goal in addition to that you can much more readily reach your goal.

Activity 4

Spend some time thinking about a time you've faced adversity.

What did you learn from it?

How have you become a better person as a result?

Step 2 - Self

Lesson 1 - Stepping Into Self-Acceptance

The better you know yourself, the better your relationship with the rest of the world

Toni Collette

Self-acceptance is being able to recognise who we are in every moment and circumstance. That doesn't mean that we always like ourselves, but that we can accept ourselves warts and all.

Learning self-acceptance is something that is closely related to what we'll cover in lesson two, but it is really the basis of having a healthy relationship with yourself, and as the quote above says having a better relationship with the rest of the world too!

As an introvert, it can feel like such a burden and bad thing that we aren't as out-going and gregarious as extroverts, but the more that we can acknowledge and come to terms with the fact that we are just not going to be that way, the more that we can work with our personality to get to where we want to go.

Part of being an introvert is the fact that we take longer to process our thoughts and when you understand that this is because of the way that our brains are wired, you can stop beating yourself up for it and find strategies to give yourself more time to think when you are asked a question or put on the spot.

Self-acceptance is the key to making peace with our weaknesses as well as our strengths and the choices that we make.

It's easy to compare ourselves to extroverts and find ourselves lacking, especially when they are more vocal, seem to have so much more energy in crowds and can seemingly talk to anyone!

It's also easy to put ourselves down for spending more time thinking through and not wanting to be around people all the time.

The truth is that this is a part of our personality and not something to be judged, there's nothing wrong with us! This applies even to the bits we don't like and we think are flawed.

When we can fully accept ourselves though, we can see that we are perfectly imperfect and are then more able to take action to do our best and better ourselves. Not in a way that says I am not enough or inadequate so I need to fix myself, but in a way that says I understand myself enough to know how to get my needs met. One example of coping is to let people know that you'll need a break from the party and recharge on your own. Another is to let people know that you need more time to prepare answers to questions or come up with ideas and solutions so knowing the meeting agenda beforehand will help.

It gives us a way to make sure that we ask for what we need and take care of ourselves with compassion.

A key to really accepting yourself is to know the difference between being shy and being an introvert. In its true form introversion is about being focused internally vs extroversion which is about being focused externally.

It is more about where your energy goes in order to recharge. As an introvert that usually means that you need time alone or in a quiet space with only a few other people to regain your energy. Extroverts typically need the opposite in order to recharge or more accurately gain energy from lots of stimulation. So, they will usually be found surrounded by lots of people and noise. As introverts though, we can typically be found in more understated environments with fewer people.

Being an introvert or extrovert is not a binary, on/off state. It's something that we are born into, a little bit like being male or female. There have been studies that show that introvert brains react differently to extrovert brains and that different neural pathways (circuits in the brain) are activated in different personalities.

The fact that it appears to take introverts longer to process or think of words when talking out loud is because there is a longer neural pathway that is activated and used in the brain when compared to the shorter pathway for extroverts.

Being shy is something that can affect both introverts and extroverts. Shyness is more about feeling awkward, worried or tense in social situations, typically with unfamiliar people.

At a party, a shy person may for example find it difficult to start a conversation with people they don't know. An introvert however may not mind talking to new people, but will after a certain amount of time need to take a break and either leave or retreat to a quieter space.

Mary Jane was a shy introvert in the past and struggled both to have conversations with people and to manage her energy when she was younger. She used to not enjoy parties or social situations. It wasn't until she got over her shyness that she realised she enjoyed talking to people, but found it draining after a while. Even the most active of extroverts still feel drained in social situations too!

As an introvert, you may feel like finding social situations draining is a burden because you react differently to other people around you. In fact, your introversion makes you a wonderful person to talk to at social gatherings!

Being an introvert, you likely think deeply about what you say before you say it, and that means that often you can have a perspective that is different to those around you.

This difference in perspective is something that can lead to innovation and new ideas. Some of the most innovative companies have had introverts at the helm - Apple, Dyson, Facebook to name just a few.

Your introversion also means that you listen deeply to what people say when they talk to you. This helps them to feel understood and can help them to deal with any problems and maybe even come up with original solutions.

When you are able embrace the fact that you are different, it becomes much easier to manage being an introvert. Your introversion then becomes a tool to help you move closer to the life you desire, rather than a burden that moves you away from it.

The truth is that you deserve to live a life that works for you and your introversion, in a way that isn't about you becoming someone else, or even pretending to be. You can work with your personality to do this. That's why Mary Jane and Richard wanted to write this programme!

Activity 5

In your journal, write about several situations where you feel uncomfortable and others where you feel comfortable.

What are the features of each?

Lesson 2 - Stepping Into Self-Love

The most important thing I learnt in my journey was to love me

Richard Daniel Curtis

Welcome to the area of self-love, an area free of regret, of blame, of malice, of anxiety and doubts. Whilst you are here you may only think positive things about yourself, negative thoughts of self-doubt are banished.

Self-love sounds like a bit of a selfish or ego centric phrase, but this is all about a very simple and important concept.

And it relates to psychology (hurray, a bit of science!). We learn as babies that our needs will be met if we cry or that we will be calmed. This taught us to respect ourselves and is one of the fundamental basics of our secure self.

This secure self (or 'Sense of I' as Richard calls it), is the basis for a great many outwardly facing achievements. A simple example of the importance would be to think how much easier it is to go and meet a group of friends somewhere when you have exciting news to tell them. You are feeling confident, so therefore, feel more secure, your 'Sense of I' feels far more complete at that stage, so your worries or anxieties reduce.

You may feel the same feeling when you have a new job or have passed an exam, someone else has demonstrated that you are a valuable being, so as a result you feel more confident when it comes to socialising with others.

This self-security is vital, especially when faced with new situations or dealing with things that make you anxious. It's like a foundational step to being able to be outwardly confident. The more comfortable you feel about yourself, then the more comfortable you will be with dealing with those around you.

Unfortunately, it is also possible to falsely get these feelings too. This involves abuse of alcohol, drugs or sex and can easily lead to addiction. For example, a small amount of alcohol will often make people feel good about themselves. This can make them feel and appear more confident and reduce the anxiety they feel, so they continue drinking. When they do sober up, the insecurities and anxieties return, they have not dealt with the true cause – an insecure Sense of I.

This insecurity can feel paralysing to some, so it is easy to understand how this cycle of dependency can begin as a coping mechanism.

This is where self-love comes in. It's a term used to describe the ability to like yourself for who you are and taking the time to take care of yourself. Everyone uses self-love at one time or another; even the most confident people will have days where they focus on themselves and indulge in me time. These activities help them to feel more secure and let them recoup from needing to socially give all of the time.

We'll share with you a secret, even those confident people have parts of themselves that question their confidence, try to knock them down or make them feel insecure – we all have those voices. The difference is that they have found ways of finding more positives inside themselves than negatives. They'll see the bits of themselves that bring them down as areas to work on and use the positive side of their self-talk to bring these negative parts more into line with the rest of their personality. They will still be there, just not a screaming voice or a point of pain inside their heads, more a quiet voice amongst many others.

The other secret that most confident people have, is they stop comparing themselves to other people. They recognise that they are unique and that by comparing themselves to others, feeling jealous or resentful, it actually makes their insecurities worse. So, they tend not to (I say tend as everyone does it at some point), instead focussing on what makes them feel happy and secure, enjoying the moments.

Anxiety and fear are related to the future, not what is actually happening in your life now. Think about it most anxiety-driven thoughts (*they don't like me, they won't like me, I'll bore them* and so on) are related to how other people perceive you or to things that <u>could</u> happen in the future. They're not about the present moment. If you think about it, when you think of extrovert and confident people, you think of people who are fun to be with, who make others smile, who enjoy the moment. They still have days where they feel flat or exhausted, but they're not letting that fear of being judged by others or that they'll need to have a recoupment day affect what they're doing at that time. Other people will still judge others, everyone needs a 'me' day every so often – these are just facts of life, not things to be anxious about.

Now, at this point we want to tell you that you are awesome! In fact, you are better than awesome, there is no one on this planet like you. Yes, even the bits of you, that you don't like, we think are amazing because they are part of you. No one else has the same thoughts you do, no one else can judge you on what you are thinking because that's part of you, your history and experiences. Put it simply, you would be someone else without all of the good and bad bits of you, they form part of the intelligent being that is you.

Now anything you can do (within reason) to make yourself feel more awesome helps to make you feel more confident.

But underneath that is another need, a more fundamental need that causes many difficulties associated with introversion, insecurity. It's like a parasite that niggles away at you, day and night, and the problem is that when you try to shut it out, it grows bigger.

There are two ways of dealing with these parasites, the first is to become so secure in other areas of your life it doesn't matter and the second is to look the parasites in the mirror, study them and accept them. Certainly, that's a big step we've both made in our lives.

Taking the time to understand the things you don't like about yourself, your 'demons' and where they come from is a hugely valuable exercise. But only if you then work through reframing them into positives, without the second part of the task, the horrible monsters remain horrible. Whereas, if you focus on what positives you get as a result, you will dress that dreadful monster up in ridiculous clothes, so every time you see it you smile to yourself.

For Richard, it was accepting his disability and understanding the compassion, patience and perseverance that his eczema has made him have. Without his eczema, he wouldn't have learned those attributes.

For Mary Jane, it was accepting her introversion and understanding the insightfulness, empathy and analytical mind that gave her. Without these qualities she would not have succeeded as a coach!

Activity 6

In your journals, answer the following questions.

What are the things about yourself you don't like?

Why?

Where have they come from?

What positives do they bring to your life?

Who are you going to share this learning with?

Step 3 - Family And Social Circle

Lesson 1 - Learning To Trust

Learning to trust is one of life's most difficult tasks

Isaac Watts

Trust is a hard thing to earn and an easy thing to lose. It can take some time to get to know someone, to understand their views, learn to accept them and then feel safe enough to share you with them. Deciding whether to trust someone in the first place can be a hard decision.

It all goes back to our 'Sense of I', how secure we feel about ourselves. The more secure we feel about ourselves, then the more likely it is that we will be able to make appropriate judgement calls about trusting other people. If you are anxious, under pressure or feeling insecure about something, then you are likely to either place too must trust in people and tell someone too much, only to be burnt later, or feel paranoid and not trust anyone, trying to deal with everything yourself.

Unfortunately, both can be bad for us, but finding that middle ground can be hard, let alone combined with living with introversion.

Let's explore each of the factors involved: self-security, building relationships and opening up to other people.

Feeling comfortable in your skin is important as we have already discussed. Recognising who you are, warts and all, helps you to make informed decisions about what you share and what you don't tell others. When we feel insecure or anxious, the level of cortisol (the stress drug) rises in our brain. This encourages our mammalian brain to react, making snap judgements, in order to protect us from the 'threat'. It also makes us more vigilant to things around us and puts us in a position of wanting to protect or be protected. If it's the former, then we will naturally close up, withdraw and distrust others more. If it's the latter, then our brain will be seeking for someone to offer us that protection and we're likely to seek someone to provide that for us.

We see this most with people who were abused in their early childhood. They struggle with their own self-identity and security and so often go through patterns of behaviour on two extremes.

They may distrust everyone and be fiercely independent. Why should they trust other people if other people just hurt them? Often taking a long time to trust someone in a relationship, they are hyper-cautious waiting for the time when their beliefs will be proven correct and their partner will hurt them. This in turn, makes it more likely to happen and it turns into a vicious cycle of mistrust feeding into more mistrust.

Or in the other extreme they desperately seek someone to love and feel secure with, misreading the cues and warning signs along the way and frequently (but not always) ending up in an unhealthy and damaging relationship (or series of relationships). In these cases, they are often over reliant on the other person and wouldn't know their own self-identity without the security of the relationship. Their desire to be wanted, needed and loved often puts them in the situation where they haven't learned to be comfortable with how to have a healthy relationship and hang onto it so tightly that they end up suffocating it.

Now, these are extreme examples, but you can see the link between insecurity and lack of trust in other people. It happens on lesser extents too, a friend who gossips to you about someone else makes you wonder if they gossip to others about you and so on.

Let's move onto relationship building. When a relationship initially forms it is often as a result of some kind of shared (and therefore secure) experience or interest – you are drawn to people in a social circle who share similar experiences or hold similar views to you. Mary Jane and Richard meeting in the planning for a mental health conference is a classic example of this, the friendship they have developed is as a result of a shared number of experiences growing up.

This initial meeting is then followed by a number of 'safe' activities, where the relationship grows whilst the people involved do something together. This does not just apply to romantic relationships, friends do the same, as do families with a baby – they bond by sharing a number of fun or engaging games with the infant.

Using this concept of safety, over time we learn to trust the other person, we are able to understand their values and beliefs and 'check' that they match ours before we trust them. The same is true within our family, where we will often find it easier to speak in confidence to someone who our views are aligned with, as we feel 'safe' with the responses or advice they are likely to give us.

And there are things that can result in this trust being partially or wholly lost. We see it in marriages, where the relationship 'security' is lost as it transpires one of the couple have been lying about something for a long period of time. A friendship ruined because someone stole from someone else (a physical thing or even a romantic partner).

Trust all comes from security, security in others generally comes from security in ourselves.

So now you have developed trust in someone else (or you already had it, for example in the case of a family member), let's talk about the final step – opening up.

This is often the hardest for people, introvert or not, because it involves sharing your thoughts openly. So often we filter the things we say, hold ourselves back and don't say the things we want to because the voice in our head tells us that we will be judged, disliked, put down, demonised or even lose that friend. Well, let us reassure you, that even the most outgoing confident extravert has those voices. They are a part of all of us, the difference is that some people learn to ignore or quieten them, others don't. Richard views his as a child's voice and internally reassures the voice that it will be alright, Mary Jane has learned to listen to what the voice really needs and finds ways to get that need met.

When you do open up to someone, the environment plays a part too. You don't want to be somewhere where you will be constantly interrupted or people, who you don't want to listen, can hear you – your environment needs to be safe too.

Once you have decided you need advice or support from someone, use the activity below to help identify the people you can talk to about the issue. Ask them if they can help you and arrange a time and place to have that conversation (it may be as simple as can we go somewhere quieter, to arranging to take a friend out for a meal to discuss the issue).

Silence is a vital part of opening up, but so often overlooked. As humans, we try to fill silence, we abhor it and if we're sat there trying to listen to someone, but they're not saying anything, we make suggestions about what they could say. This is unhelpful as it doesn't allow the person opening up to think through what they are trying to deal with, instead they answer the shorter follow-up questions, not what they originally wanted to speak about. We refer to it as making a decision about who owns the silence, if we asked you a question and want you to answer, then it is your silence and we are rude to interrupt it. If you need to understand the question or don't know, then you would say "I don't understand" or "I don't know" - it is your silence to own.

If you want to have a conversation with someone to help you open up or talk about an issue, then ask them to listen and not interrupt your silence whilst you work it out in your head. You can say to them that you'll ask them to help you if you are struggling, but this is your silence for you to work out what you're trying to say.

Here's a few ideas about things you could try to open up to people you trust:

> Go for a walk together and talk as you walk;
>
> Play a slow-paced game together (like chess);
>
> Do a problem-solving activity together;
>
> Make a meal with each other;
>
> Go on a long drive.

You will notice that they are all activities where you are both focused on something – many people find it easier to talk when they are not focussing on each other or the conversation.

Activity 7

On a double blank page in your journal, write your name in the centre of both pages. Label the pages "Circle of Trust"

On the left-hand page write down your family members in order of trust – the close they are to your name, the more you trust them. Draw a circle, with your name in the centre, around those you trust completely. In a different colour draw another circle including those who you trust with only some things and finally, in a different colour, a circle for people you only trust with a few things.

Repeat the exercise on the right-hand page with your friends.

Lesson 2 - Learning To Set Boundaries

Being a nice person is about courtesy: you're friendly, polite, agreeable, and accommodating. When people believe they have to be nice in order to give, they fail to set boundaries, rarely say no, and become pushovers, letting others walk all over them.

Adam Grant

We want to begin this lesson by talking to you about something called containment. This is a psychological theory developed in the 1950s primarily by a psychoanalyst called Wilfred Bion. He drew on the previous work of Melanie Klein to develop a theory of how infants learn to contain their emotions.

Bion's concept was that as babies display raw emotions, then the mother will take those emotions, process them and return them to the infant in a more digestible manner. The concept is that through this early pairing, the infant learns how to limit their emotions themselves. They learn to set emotional boundaries themselves. This is just one of many ways that parents teach an infant a sense of self-identity and self-security – they are someone whose needs will be met and that they deserve them to be met.

Over the next few years, our parents continue to give us that sense of security that they fostered in us as infants. One of the things that research has shown is important in parenting is a combination of rules, boundaries and consequences, combined with an underlying responsiveness to the needs of the child, such as explaining why the rule is there or helping them deal with the emotions of having done something in the first place.

Boundaries are important to humans, they give us a sense of where the line is, where to stop ourselves, what is expected of us – they give us psychological security.

You may not realise the unconscious boundaries you have in your mind, but there will be many in there telling you where to draw the line, without you necessarily realising. An example of this is when you find yourself in a back and forth argument, when you are both escalating and at some point you walk away or do something to break the emotional deadlock – your brain, consciously or unconsciously, has put in a maximum temperature and stopped you going beyond that. Some layers of boundaries protect you from threats – real and imaginary. This is incredibly helpful, for example you do not stab someone with whom you are angry, and instead you find a more reasonable way of dealing with that emotion (and saving yourself from a very hefty prison sentence).

Unconscious boundaries that protect us from imaginary threats are more concerning. Some are founded on very real threats, for example the voices telling you how long you can swim underwater, that even when you know you can hold your breath for longer, are still there telling you that you are in danger.

Other unconscious boundaries we have may show themselves as inhibitors or self-doubt. Ever looked through the job adverts and self-selected yourself out of many that would be really interesting, because you 'couldn't do them'? We do it all of the time without realising. Another example would be being able to speak to a group of more than six people (substitute any number in there) – there is nothing to suggest that they will pose more of a threat than a smaller number. In actual fact, due to the psychological theories surrounding compliance and conformity, people in larger groups are more likely to do what the group is doing (even if that involves breaking the law). So, in terms of listening to someone speak, they are far more likely to listen (even if they don't enjoy it) than they are to argue or interrupt the speaker.

Unfortunately, if you experience anxiety, then this can reinforce these unconscious boundaries or limiting beliefs. Anxiety is often linked to introversion, but it is a different beast. Anxiety can be a worry or concern over topics, events or activities that is more frequent and long term than a normal worry or concern (for diagnostic criteria it needs to be over six months) and more challenging to control. It is often linked to physical symptoms, such as edginess, restlessness, fatigue, impaired concentration, irritability, soreness or aching of the muscles, and difficulty with sleeping (too little, interrupted or restless). Anxiety is linked to the fear of something happening and can result in things like panic attacks, fear of social situations, fear of crowds or in worst-case situations fear of leaving the house. Whilst introverts may experience anxiety, if someone is experiencing long-term and life-altering anxiety we would recommend visiting a health care professional as it may be related to a clinical form of anxiety, not just being an introvert – a possible mental health condition, rather than a personality type.

For introverts, boundary setting is important, especially when it comes to those times when you will be going beyond your comfort zone. Just the same as with goal setting earlier in this programme, when you set yourself boundaries, you want to stretch yourself slightly, but not too far that you feel unsafe. At the same time you want them to be realistic boundaries, not so far away that you will feel yourself fail before you reach the boundary. Remember, unlike goals, boundaries are about protecting you.

So, when you are doing something that moves you towards your goal, then take the time to set your own boundaries for that activity. If it's going to a social function and you normally only stay for an hour, set yourself a boundary of ninety minutes, that way, even if you are succeeding then you won't push yourself too far. If it's to speak in front of a group, then make it a group you are comfortable with, plus a few additions, don't go straight to several hundred people!

Now, one of the things that could sabotage your self-established boundary is other people. We've spoken about social conformity earlier and this can affect you too. It is really important that you recognise your boundary and what measures you have in place within your social circle to stick to it (even if it means having a wing man there to prod you to go home).

Not pushing yourself too far is an important part of self-development. Earlier in this programme, we spoke about breaking large goals down into smaller achievable steps, the boundaries you set along the way will be what stops you from rushing through all of them and pushing yourself so far out of your comfort zone that you struggle to maintain it. Both introverts and extroverts need to spend time recuperating when they are involved in something like a social gathering, use boundaries that you set to make sure that this happens for you.

Activity 8

Revisit the target you set in Activity 2. On a scale of 0-10 (0 being not moving) rate how you are moving towards this goal.

Write a list of all of the things that are interfering with you moving forwards towards your goal (for example, not devoting time, other people's views, fear of how other people will react).

Now, on another scale of 0-10 rate how big an impact these factors are having on you achieving your goal (0 – no impact, I'm flying, 10 – I'm at a standstill, too many things are in the way).

Spend a few minutes writing down the boundaries you could put in place in order to reduce the impact these things are having on you achieving your goal.

Lesson 3 - Feeling Safe To Ask

If you don't ask, the answer is always no

Nora Roberts/ Tony Robbins

When we don't feel safe to ask for what we need or desire then very often we can end up feeling frustrated and unloved because the people around us may not always notice that we are distressed or in need of help.

It can feel like a very vulnerable thing to do, to ask for help or support or simply for something that we need, but when we have taken the time to develop relationships with people we trust and set healthy boundaries it gets much easier.

When it comes to asking for support there are a few broad groups of people that you might turn to, to ask for what you need.

The first is your family. Depending on the kind of relationship you have with your family, you may find this an easier group of people to turn to for support.

The second is your friends. For some of you, you may find that it is easier to ask for what you need from friends.

The final broad group is people in positions of responsibility. That could include teachers, doctors, nurses, religious leaders, counsellors, bank managers, investors, basically people that have something that you need that you don't know very well.

The first step to asking for what you need is to get clear about what that may be and then think about which of these groups of people may be able to help you.

If you need help studying for an exam is there anyone in your family or group of friends you could ask for help or would you prefer to hire a tutor?

If you need relationship advice would you feel more comfortable and able to receive good advice from a family member, a friend or a relationship expert?

Clearly it depends on what kind of support you are looking for. Often friends and family can give more supportive, sympathetic support, but perhaps not the best advice, whereas an external expert may be able to give more sound advice. They may be more detached and professional than a family member or friend though.

You may find that you prefer to turn to different people depending on the type of support that you need, that's perfectly fine. When Mary Jane had an unexpected bereavement in 2017 she turned to friends and family in the immediate aftermath, but found that it was helpful to get external support as well. In his late 20s Richard suffered with depression, went through a relationship breakup and was struggling to perform at work. With the help of a strong circle of friends and some short-term counselling, Richard learned to put some of the things making him anxious into a new perspective and make decisions that ultimately led to him moving into the behaviour field.

Whoever you decide to turn to for support, it is vital to be able to communicate clearly what you need and it also helps if the people you turn to understand what you are looking for.

If you know that you prefer to have someone listen to what you say before they jump in with solutions and suggestions, then it may be helpful to let the person you've turned to for support know that you just need them to listen to you first, before they suggest anything. This is a good thing for us to do when talking to our friends or partners as they may want to rush in with a solution when all we really need is for them to listen.

Maybe you know that you need support in getting clear about what to do in a certain situation and that what you really need is someone to ask you questions that help you get there.

Maybe you need a shoulder to cry on and a hug and no words have to be spoken at all.

Whatever it is that you need no one else is ultimately responsible for meeting that need except you. Your family and friends, teachers, colleagues and mentors/advisors can support you, but it is important for you to learn what is best for you and communicate that clearly with the people around you to make sure that you get your needs met.

This is as much about you being a good communicator and asking, as it is about you understanding the best way to speak to and ask those around you for support. No one way of asking for support will work for you and every single person that you meet.

When it comes to asking for help here are some things that you might like to try:

> Choose a time to ask when you are both relaxed and perhaps are alone.

> Be as specific as you can about what you are asking for and when you need it by.

Think about how you can minimise the risk and cost to the person who is helping you. Don't offer something that you can't give, but let them know that you have considered the impact of what you are asking for on them. This will be different depending on who you are asking and what you are asking for. If you are asking for time to talk about something and you know that the person you'd like to support you is short on time, perhaps asking them to support you in advance can allow your supporter or potential supporter to choose a time that works for them.

Be open to compromising and let them know how urgent your need for help is.

If you know you have an urgent need it may be worth considering a few people who may be able to help you, and that you would feel comfortable asking.

When it comes to helping others to understand you, as an introvert it will be helpful to spend time with people you think could be good friends and support you to develop the trust necessary to ask for support. This takes time and being vulnerable and asking for help is a great way to build deeper trust and relationships with people.

It is also helpful to have good boundaries too which we have covered earlier. In fact often being able to get support relies on our and our supporter's healthy boundaries. Part of both asking for support and having healthy boundaries is being clear about what you need, so before approaching someone for support take the time to get clear about what you are asking for.

Sometimes it may not be possible to be clear without talking to someone and getting support so consider if there are people that you can turn to for support to do that. If you struggle to talk to someone you could always use a journal to jot things down and think things through.

When you take the time to get clear on your needs and the support you require it is much easier to get those needs met!

Activity 9

Revisit your Circles of Trust from Activity 7, who are the people who will turn to for support on your journey? Remember, it doesn't need to be someone you've turned to before – sometimes a fresh opinion is exactly what you need to move forward.

What are you going to ask them?

How could they react?

How *will* they react? (Be honest with yourself here, it's likely to be different than the previous answer.)

Step 4 - How The World Sees You

Activity 10

On a double page in your journal, write down on one side, how you think the world perceives you. Make sure you include areas of your life like:

Personality

Social skills

Outlook

Passion and drive

Meeting new people

Just focus on your perception of how they see you, we'll come to how to they actually perceive you (which is often very different) later once we've gone through some other bits. Leave the other side blank as this is the space you'll need for Activity 12.

Lesson 1 - How To Accept Feedback

Each person does see the world in a different way. There is not a single, unifying, objective truth. We're all limited by our perspective

Siri Hustvedt

A boy grows up in a village at the base of a mountain, he marries a woman from the village and they start a family. He works in the fields on the outskirts of the village and has no need to leave the settlement. One day a visitor arrives in the village, he is a fisherman from a village on the coast several miles away. They begin talking and the fisherman tells the farmer about this amazing world where there are flat fields for miles available for growing crops, villages and towns. "Why haven't I heard of this place?" asks the farmer. "Have you never wondered what is beyond the mountain?" replies the fisherman.

People know what they know and see what they see – perception is everything. Perception is very much based on own experience, our past and our beliefs. Jean Piaget, a psychologist, developed a problem called the Three Mountain Problem to understand the development of perspective. On a table, there are three different sized mountains, one topped with snow, another a hut and another a red cross. He asked different aged children to look at the model, then place a doll on one side of the model. The children would then be sat down and shown a series of pictures from the different sides and asked them to identify which was the view the doll had. This experiment has been repeated in a number of different ways over the years, but allows us to consider the importance of understanding different viewpoints.

The proverb about the glass being half empty or half full is also a classic example of perception. Depending on your outlook, or mindset, then you will approach it differently. Interestingly, there is a recent view developing that people who ask themselves how they will achieve something may outperform those who merely believe they are going to achieve something.

In this step we are going to be taking you on a journey to think about how other people see you and using that to make you the person you want to be. It is important to be comfortable with how others see you and how you see yourself. We covered self-love earlier in the programme, but now we want you to be comfortable with how others perceive you.

Perception is really important when considering feedback. People will say things from their point of view and just as we've explained above, this is taken from their experience, past and beliefs. Here's just a few things that will affect the way someone perceives someone else:

> Their mood;
>
> What feedback they've been given in the past;
>
> Their desire to please other people;
>
> Their own self-love (they might say what they think you want to hear so it makes them feel good);
>
> You remind them of someone else (and psychologically they then expect you to be the same);
>
> Their experiences of giving honest feedback in the past;
>
> The strength of your relationship with them (they might not want to risk damaging it).

It is important to bear this in mind when you receive any feedback, whether it is about your work, your personality, your dress sense. When you receive feedback, especially the kind you may not want to hear, deal with it in a very clinical way to begin with, some people even write it down.

Activity 11

Revisit your Circles of Trust from Activity 7, which people would give you feedback that would help you without being rude?

Write a list on one side of a double page in your journal of people who would give you feedback and note next to each things that would affect their perception.

Asking for feedback on how others perceive us can trigger some fear responses within us. There's the fear of not being liked (not everyone can like us), there's the fear of people seeing who we really are (we all have that), the fear of people judging us (everyone does at some point) and the fear that they'll be unkind and hurt us (we all want to protect ourselves from harm). Let's be honest, asking people about how you come across is scary.

However, on this journey of self-discovery we feel it is vital that you learn about how other perceive you. In an ideal world, the feedback you receive is aligned to how you see yourself – you have external validation for your internal perception. What is more common is that you have some areas of alignment and others where the external perception is slightly different from where you want to be. There is nothing wrong with that, unless it is widely different and you are strongly opposed to how you are viewed by others.

If we do find that we are strongly conflicting with how people perceive aspects of our lives, then we have a choice – we either establish that as a part of our personality that other people need to put up with, or we make a decision to change.

Changing the way we are, or the way we act, is not an overnight thing – you are effectively rewiring your brain, so can take weeks or months to settle into a new behaviour. It begins with a decision, to be more grateful to people for example, moves into deciding the new behaviour (to say thank you more often) and then into enacting the new behaviour (saying thank you more often). After a few days this decision becomes less important in your mind as you are trying to get on with your life, and you have to force yourself to remember to do the new behaviour. You start kicking yourself and telling yourself you are never going to change it, so you start resisting against your own new regime, your brain almost takes pride in the fact that you are alright even though you haven't carried out your own promise (for example diets!).

This is the hardest part of behaviour change – forcing yourself to keep going. Once you get through this bit, you find the new behaviour starts to almost become automatic – you start thanking people in the shop for things randomly or feel strange not saying it – this is because you have entrenched the new behaviour.

The behaviour change process really can take time, including several false starts normally. So write yourself sticky notes and affix them to the mirror, to the computer, in fact anywhere you look for long periods of time, to remind yourself of this decision and to help you get through that frustrating depressive bit in the middle.

Activity 12

Ask the people you have listed in Activity 11 about their perceptions of the areas you listed in Activity 10. Use the blank space opposite that list from Activity 10 to write down their responses.

Highlight the areas that match.

Finally, write down by the side of these lists, how you would like to be perceived in each of the areas.

Lesson 2 - How To Adjust Misperceptions

Not caring more about what other people think than what you think. That's freedom.

Demi Moore

Not everyone you know or meet will totally get and understand you. Not everyone will like you.

When it comes to your goals and putting yourself out there, people may judge you as being something or someone that you are not. Mary Jane and Richard are both frequently mistaken for extroverts when speaking.

In order to achieve your goals, you will need to put yourself out there and take the risk, in spite of what other people may or may not think!

People form perceptions based on their own experiences, knowledge and biases. It is very easy to misunderstand someone from a perception that is made in the spur of the moment.

When you meet someone in person for the first time, in a matter of moments you will have formed an impression of that person based on not just what they have said and how, but also their body language, what they wear and how they sound.

It can be very easy to misunderstand something you have perceived. That's why it's a challenge when there are witnesses to a crime. They may have seen something that they didn't totally understand or that didn't really happen and why it is important for there to be more than one witness.

As humans we are meaning making machines and the meanings we assign to behaviours depends on our experiences and what we've decided the behaviour means in the past.

Optical illusions are a great way to illustrate the idea of perceptions and misunderstandings that can arise.

A famous illusion is one of two faces or a vase. What you see depends on what part you focus on, and if someone else is focusing on a different part to you they will see something different and a misunderstanding occurs.

In life this can happen with any communication, action or movement that we can see and interpret. The part that we are focused on informs what we see and what meanings we attach to that.

As we go through life our biology and experiences shape how we see things. If we are colour blind we may see certain colours differently to everyone else and wonder what they are on about, but when we can realise and accept that other people see things differently then we can start to realise that it isn't personal and what we may need to do to be understood and liked.

As an introvert our need for time alone to recharge is often mistaken for being shy, but when we can understand ourselves we can explain that to people so they don't take it personally or think it's them.

Of course, not everyone will understand or like you, and that is OK! Famous brands like Apple, Amazon, Google or your favourite celebrities are not liked by everyone!

The key is being able to distinguish the people who are your fans, or your tribe, versus the people who aren't.

The former group will be those who will support and encourage you, listen and understand you or at least put in the effort to. That isn't to say they will always have nice things to say, but when giving feedback they make sure it's constructive and helpful and doesn't make you wrong, bad or stupid.

The latter will be people who rather than build you up, cut you down. They may not do this actively, by calling you names or criticising you, but those who allow others to tear you down without coming to your aid are not really on your side either.

It's a good idea to know who you feel you can turn to for support and who you don't feel you can. Be mindful that there is a difference between someone who sees things from a different perspective, but supports you and someone who doesn't. The former will make an effort to share their thoughts with you in a supportive way whereas the latter may not bother.

It might seem at first glance that someone with a different perspective isn't supporting you, but if you can be open to hearing the different perspective it may give you a new way of doing things that is more effective.

Perceptions can shift when you gain more information or understanding about a particular topic. Mary Jane often didn't understand why her teachers were always encouraging her to speak up in class until she became a speaker and realised it was about making sure the content was understood.

As a very insecure teenager, Richard was frightened to make friends and would distance himself from his peers in order to avoid being bullied. He perceived the actions of other teens as intimidation or aggressiveness. Many years later, one of those other teens is now one of his best friends. They long ago had the conversation about the different perspectives on those teenage actions that Richard thought were designed to emotionally hurt him. He learned that his friend was dealing with a very tough time of his own during that period and had no idea how he was making Richard feel.

This is something to be aware of when other people are getting to know or approach you, they may have a perception of you that is inaccurate that you may need to adjust by sharing more information with them or spending more time with them. Often people will make assumptions based on their perceptions of you and unless you are aware of it, you cannot take the necessary steps to adjust them, assuming of course that you want to!

When it comes to your goals sometimes it can seem like you are moving away from your goals rather than toward them, but when you stop and think about it the information, lessons and feedback you have gained actually help you to get even clearer about where you want to go.

Mary Jane's goal when she was younger was to be happy. When she quit her job to start her business, there were times when she felt really unhappy, like when she had to go out networking to promote her business, but learning to network effectively is part of what has led her to where she is today!

Richard takes the view that every day he will take a step closer to his goals – even if it is a step back. There are times in setting up a business that you can end up in a dead end, and in order to move forward you need to take a step back. For every decision or demand on his time, Richard asks himself "will it move me towards or away from where I am headed?" This simple 2 second sanity check has led to Richard passing on some business opportunities and moving forward with others, even if it is at a very slow pace.

Take a look at your goals and take a moment to think about if you feel you are moving toward or away from them. If you feel you are moving away from your goal, ask yourself if there is something you can learn from your experience that may be able to help you.

Correcting misunderstandings of perception is not an easy task, so some things you can try are as follows:

For correcting your own perceptions:

> Ask yourself what can/did I learn from this experience? Where can I get more information to find out what I am missing?

For correcting other's perceptions:

> Work out if the misperception is important to you. Only correct it if you feel that it will have a negative impact on your relationship or your development.

> Try to understand where the other person is coming from, use your empathy and listening skills and see if you can use that information to help the other person see your perspective.

Activity 13

On a fresh page in your journal (with nothing on the back), write a list of the people who you feel hold you back (even yourself if you feel you hold yourself back at times).

Beside each one write down what they do that holds you back.

Now, write down how each person makes you feel.

Finally, rip the page from your journal and destroy it – you don't deserve that negativity in your life!

Step 5 - Other People

Lesson 1 - How To Communicate

No Man is an Island

John Donne

The saying is never truer, in the modern world we are dependent on other people. Even if you live alone and don't go out, you need to rely on others to deliver your groceries. For the introvert, this can be one of the biggest causes of stress, how to effectively communicate with others when secretly you like your own company.

Many introverts learn the basics of effective communication and deploy them as a coping mechanism for social situations. Tactics like having a firm handshake, holding your head up when meeting people and making good eye contact are things they learn to compensate for their introversion. These help people to feel safe with you and relate back to that self-security we spoke about earlier. Ever had a conversation with someone where you didn't quite get them or you felt uncomfortable? It was probably related with them emitting some kind of threat or a mismatch between their different communication styles (for example their speech and their body language).

Communication is the act of transmitting and receiving information, it can include verbal, non-verbal, visual and written.

Let's go through the key skills related to verbal communication:

> Speaking
>
> Listening
>
> Empathy
>
> Questioning
>
> Making conversations
>
> Small-talk

Accompanying or replacing verbal skills are non-verbal skills, these include:

> Eye contact
>
> Facial expressions
>
> Body language
>
> Gestures
>
> Tone and pitch of voice
>
> Touch
>
> Physical distance from speaker/listener

Written communication can include:

> Reports
>
> Emails
>
> Texts
>
> Books

And finally visual communication can include:

> Signs
>
> Posters
>
> Diagrams
>
> Images
>
> Emoji's

It is important that the forms of communication match, otherwise, as described earlier, it may be picked up by others as an insincerity or cause them to subconsciously interpret it as a threat. At an animalistic level, we are subconsciously checking for these cues to make sure that we don't need to run away, freeze or hide.

There are a number of things the second communication method could show. Ideally it will repeat or match the message being given, an example is when someone says they are excited about something and their body language shows that they are jumping up and down. In a more formal context, there might be a new procedure spoken about at a staff meeting, which is then repeated in a memo to all staff.

Alternatively the second form of communication may show contradictory behaviour, such as when someone says they don't mind volunteering for a task, but hangs their head low, with the shoulders dropped and stood at the back of the room. In advanced psychological practice this second form can also be used to cause confusion and cover up some form of deceit. Substitution is another alternative, where a verbal word is replaced with a gesture, for example "would you like a [drinking motion]?"

Two other secondary forms of communication are complementing, where another form of communication emphasises what is being said – for example a shoulder shrug accompanying the phrase "I have no idea what he's doing!" Accenting is when you use another form of communication to emphasise just part of a message, for example gesturing, slowing down speech, stamping a foot, or even bringing the word up on screen as it is said. Secondary forms of communication can also be used in deceiving people to back up your point, for example an over-exaggerated gesture when saying "I didn't do it!"

Now, when it comes to someone who is not comfortable in the environment they are in, for example a social gathering, it is very easy for their non-verbal communication to be screaming discomfort rather than matching what they are saying (unless they are saying how uncomfortable they feel). This is a familiar feeling for many introverts, who have often summoned together a great deal of guts to be there in the first place. Going with people you are comfortable would help, for example having a wing man or woman to be there as you speak to people. Some people we know who are anxious in social situations will direct their talk at someone they know, even if speaking to a stranger to help overcome this.

A good example of where primary and secondary communication sources don't always match is in our power statement. A power statement is 2-3 sentences that introduce you and what you are trying to achieve, here's ours, see if you can tell whose is whose:

My mission is to change the lives of a generation of people around the globe. I do this by helping others to understand how to listen, understand and communicate with others, whether it be adults or children.

My mission is to empower people to move toward their dreams. I do this by supporting introvert entrepreneurs to grow thriving businesses.

When you write your power statement, make sure you practice saying it and writing it. You have to be able to express it in multiple ways with ease. Practice saying it to yourself, practice with friends, family, the cat, practice in the car, when walking the dog. Most importantly, you need to make sure you have learnt it and can recite it to yourself in front of a mirror or camera, so you can check that your secondary communication methods are backing up what your words are saying.

Activity 14

In your journal write a list of the 3-5 things you want to include in your power statement.

Now, draft that into 2-3 sentences introducing the new you – memorise this.

Finally, stand in front of a full length mirror every day, look yourself in the eye and recite your power statement 5 times, starting quietly and getting louder and more confident each time you say it.

Lesson 2 - Dealing With Other People's Emotions

He who knows others is wise; he who knows himself is enlightened.

Lao Tzu

When you build relationships with other people, at some point, you'll find yourself dealing with some sort of emotion, whether that's a good feeling like happiness or love or a more negative one like anger or jealousy. How you deal with emotions is a vital key to making sure that your relationships work for you and continue to support you.

Of course it is easier to build relationships on good emotions like happiness and joy and gratitude, but the real skill comes when you confront the more negative ones.

Emotions are a natural part of being human. We all experience some basic emotions and there is some evidence that animals also experience emotions.

Dealing with emotions starts with not making them wrong. When we deny our own (and other's) emotions we can make it much more difficult to cope with them. The more that we can learn to accept them and allow them the faster they pass through.

In early 2017 Mary Jane experienced the unexpected loss of a close family friend who was staying at her home. During that time there were a lot of negative emotions that she experienced, like fear, shock, grief, anger and sadness. The more that she denied the negative emotions the harder things felt. When she got support and allowed her emotions to be expressed she very quickly moved through her grief.

Over the years Richard has worked in some very intense environments, such as mental health units and on ambulances. Often, a way of coping for workers in these sectors, is to put your head down and keep going. So when faced with children displaying challenging behaviour, this was the way Richard acted – he didn't want to be seen as weak. Two Educational Psychologists, Alyce and Anne, worked with Richard's team to help them recognise their own emotions and how that was affecting the children's behaviours. They made it alright to feel those emotions and that it wasn't a sign of weakness.

Learning to cope with your own emotions is the first step to being able to effectively manage other people's emotions, even though not everyone will react in the same way that we do with the same emotions, or feel the same emotions in similar situations, understanding how emotions work for us gives us a good basis to have an idea of how others feel and what they may need to cope with them.

It also allows us to cope better when in highly emotional situations, like arguments or in uncomfortable and challenging ones like when we talk to others about our boundaries and needs.

When it comes to dealing with emotions, both our own and those of others, validating them can go a long way. Recognise them, name them, you are allowed to feel, that's not wrong. Don't make yourself or someone else feel bad for your feelings.

When Mary Jane was dealing with her grief a grief counsellor helped her to see that of course she would feel the way that she did given what had happened and her earlier life experience. This gave her both external and internal validation, which made it much easier for her to cope with the heavy, negative emotions she was experiencing at the time.

When we feel bad about having our emotions we tend to deny or ignore them, which means that we waste a lot of energy trying to squash them down. In the end this doesn't work, because frequently there comes a point when we'll snap, one small thing sets us off into a rage causing more damage than simply allowing and validating our emotions when we experience them.

Some safe ways of dealing with negative emotions are to journal, talk to a friend or a therapist or do some vigorous exercise. Mary Jane found cycling, yoga and salsa dancing are great ways for her to vent her frustrations through exercise. Richard practises (and has written about) Gratitude, he switches everything off and spends time playing with his baby son, or he immerses himself in a complex jigsaw puzzle.

When you are clearer about your own emotions and can handle them well, it becomes much easier to allow others to have emotions and not to take them on ourselves. It can be tempting to try to fix it when someone else is sad or angry, and often it's not helpful to provide solutions until that person is ready for them. The easiest way to know if they are ready for support is to ask them!

It's easier to create some distance with the emotions of other people when we realise that what other people feel isn't really about us. It's really about the other person and what is going on for them right now.

Have you ever had one of those days where everything just seemed to be going wrong? You missed the bus or train to work or school, you spilled coffee on your shirt and your project was a flop. Then when you got home your partner/mum got on your case about tidying your room and you get annoyed and slam the door.

Was the bad mood really caused by someone asking you to tidy your room? Or was it because it felt like the entire day was one thing after another that didn't go right?

It's the same for other people. Very often how we react to a situation isn't about what is happening in this moment right now. Usually it's a reaction to the memory of similar situations where perhaps things didn't go as planned or wanted, and the more that we can realise this, allow for it and accept it; the more that we can see that what happens in a situation isn't just down to us. While we are definitely in charge of our experience and reactions, we are not in charge of anyone else's so knowing it isn't all about us whatever the situation, can help us to find the space to allow and validate the other person's emotions and to choose how we'd like to respond.

Mastering and being in charge of your emotions and experience, isn't about controlling your emotions or other people, but ultimately about understanding, allowing and accepting them. When we can do that, then change becomes inevitable and easy. When we deny or fight against our emotions or other people's change feels like an uphill battle that ultimately ends in defeat.

When it comes to the emotions of those close to us, we can unconsciously pick them up and think they are ours, the best way to make sure that we stay in charge of our experience is to take the time to process and allow any and all of the emotions that we feel.

Great ways to do that are:

> Journaling
>
> A talking therapy or counselling
>
> Talking to an understanding friend
>
> Vigorous exercise

Not so great ways to deal with emotions include violence against animals or other people, over eating, over indulging in alcohol or drugs, or generally anything that numbs us to our feelings. This is tricky because it is so very tempting to squash down and ignore things that we don't want to feel or deal with, and what usually happens is that they will come out in indirect ways if we don't confront them immediately. Don't worry if you find that it is too much or too hard to deal with on your own. Get support and know that it is not easy for anyone, but it is doable!

Activity 15

Think about a time that someone has pushed their emotions onto you and you were left with that emotion (for example anger or embarrassment).

Now think about a time that someone tried to push their emotions onto you, but you didn't get left with their emotions.

What made it different?

What are the things you can do to put up a defence barrier against those emotions?

Finally, write a list of activities you find help you to release any negative or unwanted emotions you do pick up.

Step 6 - Peak Performance

Lesson 1 - What Is Success?

Self-belief and hard work will always earn you success

Virat Kohli

Success is an important part of personal development, recognising it is vital. Recognising success may involve noticing the things you do, say or think automatically (subconsciously). It could be completing a series of activities, it might be beating your own performance at a task you've done before or it may be doing something for the first time. Whichever it is, when you are setting a goal, take a moment to think about how you will know you have made it.

Remember back in Step 1 we spoke about dopamine and how useful it is to help us to keep going, but at the same time, too much can send us into a dopamine loop. The same is true about goals and success. If we focus on moving from one goal to the next goal, to the next, without stopping to recognise and celebrate our successes, then you will find yourself in a dopamine loop, constantly seeking the next step, the next goal to achieve.

This then can lead to the person not feeling the enjoyment they set out to get or feel less positive emotions. The hedonic treadmill effect we spoke about earlier can lead to that searching journey become a 'norm' for the person on it, so they stop looking for the success and keep looking for the journey. Likewise, some people may experience anhedonia, which is a loss of interest in activities which used to be enjoyable, for similar reasons. Remembering to celebrate our successes is obviously important.

Stopping to celebrate our success also gives us other benefits. For starters, it gives us a chance to reflect on our journey. As we go through a journey of personal growth, we will discover things about ourselves and also the way we learn. It's only by pausing that we get to take stock of these and that we can properly have a chance to think about the things we have learnt and how we can use them to help us move forward in the future.

This is also a good chance to enjoy the celebration, whether it be with your closest friends or alone, it's nice sometimes to bask in the moment. That personal satisfaction is not selfish, but your reward for the effort and perseverance you have put in. Let the endorphins flow and enjoy the sensation – let's be honest there are many things in our daily life to challenge and stress us, if there's a moment to be enjoyed, we should take it.

Resting is an important part of a self-development journey, but not too much! The risk is that once you stop, you become complacent in that moment and stay there (a bit like having a few weeks off the gym and telling yourself you don't need to go back).

Finally, the other advantage of stopping is that by relaxing it gives your brain a chance to breathe and come up with new ideas. They say the most fertile field is a rested field and that is true of the human brain. Talk to any really successful business person, they will tell you that their breaks are important and often it's where they come up with their best ideas. This is because (once you get past the need to check your phone every few minutes), you start to relax and the cortisol and dopamine that have kept you going begin to reduce. This makes it easier for your brain to think more creatively, rather than focus on survival or the fight to move forward.

For you as an individual, pausing along the journey allows you to embed the new behaviours and habits into your daily lives. The change process in human behaviour can take weeks or months to embed into a habit that happens without you thinking about it. Sometimes in the desire to move forward, people think they have embedded a new habit, only for it to be forgotten three weeks later as they focus on a new habit. The truth is if this happens it wasn't embedded into your subconscious brain, you required your conscious brain to think about it in order to perform it.

Whether you are on a journey of personal, work or academic success, it is important that you take the time to appreciate the wins you are making and plan mini-celebrations for the steps along the way. We are taking you on a journey of self-discovery and along the way we would hope that you are celebrating the milestones you are making.

Firstly, it is important that as you set yourself the smaller goals leading up to the bigger one, you understand how you will know that you have succeeded at each. If this isn't clear, you need to go back to them and make them so transparent that it is easy for you to feel and experience that success. Success shouldn't need much thinking about, it should be a level that you are clear in your mind that you are working towards and that you will rest when you get there. For the mountaineer, it's making it to that next ledge (especially when they feel themselves lagging) and taking the time to look back and view the journey they have gone on so far. Repeat this again and again, they eventually get to the top without thinking about how they must climb the whole mountain. If you aren't clear about your journey goals now, go back and revisit Activity 2.

Now, we would also hope that you recognise how you celebrate your small successes. Maybe for you it's a duvet evening, or a takeaway. For some it's a trip to an art gallery or a museum, for others it's going to their favourite coffee shop and getting the hot chocolate with all of the toppings. These aren't major things, but rewards more suited to small goals along the journey.

Although a larger journey is never truly finished (we don't ever think of our personal development as being complete), it is important again to recognise the major milestones and how you will reward yourself at these times. This is likely to be something more memorable and significant, maybe it's going on a particular trip buying new clothes or planning a social gathering. Whatever it is, it should be something that is within your comfort zone, but is big enough that you will push through the pain to complete the journey and get there.

Activity 16

Once you have finished working through this programme, you deserve to celebrate your movement forward in your journey. Spend 30 minutes planning your celebration activity, whether it's going to the cinema with friends, having a meal together or just treating yourself to something special. Remember, you will deserve it!

Lesson 2 - How To Succeed

All our dreams can come true if we have the

courage to pursue them

Walt Disney

Whatever your idea of success is, on your journey to attain it you will likely encounter niggling voices both internal and external that may hold you back, especially if you aren't aware of them.

Our hope is that by preparing you for these voices you will be able to recognise them for what they are and find ways to effectively manage them.

The voices may say something like, "Are you sure...?", "Who am I to want/do/be/have___?", "Can I really...?", "Do I deserve___?"

This is the voice of doubt. Doubt kills more dreams than failure does as the quote goes.

It can sound quite reasonable and that's what makes it dangerous because then we give in to the doubt! We believe that we aren't good enough/ready/experienced or whatever your flavour of this is and that means that we are vulnerable to allow the doubt and underlying fear to keep us stuck.

Doubt can also sound like, "I don't have the time/money/energy", "I don't know enough", "I don't want to".

Learning to distinguish this voice from the truth and from what will bring you closer to your goals is a key part of not allowing the doubts to stop you. You may find that you get distracted by your doubts, at least a few times before you realise what is happening, and that is where it is important to get support to stay on track with your goal.

In fact we're sure that there were things that you wanted to achieve in the past, but because you doubted your ability to achieve them, they didn't happen and conversely when you had faith in yourself you were able to reach and achieve your goal.

Recognising doubt and nipping it in the bud, as soon as you notice it is the best way to make sure that you stay on track to reaching your goals.

That could look like positive affirmations, which take your negative doubtful thoughts and changes them into more positive helpful ones. So for example if one of your doubts is "I never have enough money", you might like to replace it with "I have more than enough money". It may feel uncomfortable and artificial at first, and if you struggle to believe the direct opposite of your belief try to change it to something more believable.

In the case of the doubt "I never have enough money", the more direct opposite would be "I always have enough money", but that may not feel true or possible so "I have more than enough money" may work better.

Then this positive affirmation can be something you use first thing in the morning and whenever you become aware of that particular doubt.

When you start to become aware of your doubts you may over time start to notice that you waste less time procrastinating and have more energy to get things done. As introverts we spend a lot of time in our heads and our thoughts, so it can be especially helpful if the mental environment we create is a positive one!

It is important to make sure that you take care of your energy levels and manage your time well. As an introvert that will mean that you schedule in time to recharge from activities with alone / quiet time and make sure to get enough sleep as well as eat well and exercise.

This will support you to make sure you stay healthy not just in body and mind, but also in your finances as well. It's hard to reach your goal if you are feeling sick, are down and have no money. It's not impossible, but it does take more time than if you are healthy, feeling happy and have some money to support yourself with!

Making sure to take time to recharge and de-stress will not only help you to stay healthy in body and mind but it will also counter intuitively help you to make more money. This is because having more energy will mean that you can do more work when you work, and feeling good tends to bring more opportunities your way.

Richard's work takes him all over the globe and it is very easy to get caught up in 12 or 14 hour days. However, he very firmly believes that this can only be achieved by taking care of his own mental wellbeing. Having experienced depression and felt suicidal at times, he knows just what the bottom feels like and has developed a number of tactics to ensure that he doesn't become overwhelmed. For starters, Richard will make sure that he visits a spa about once a month, even if for only half a day, to dump his phones and relax his body and his mind. Each day Richard will also spend time practising Gratitude – the act of saying or writing down the things that he is grateful for at that time. Even on long days, Richard will take an hour to unwind before going to bed so that he doesn't go to bed worrying.

When Mary Jane was coping with grief in early 2017 she stayed healthy, but was understandably emotionally low and running her business was a bit of a struggle. Talks got cancelled and business ground to a halt. Later in the year when she had more energy and was happier her business became much easier to run. She did more talks and got more clients.

As you can see the three healths (mind, body and money) are intimately linked and a change in one will affect a change in the others, so it is vital to be able to maintain health in all three arenas. This will not be a static thing. Like life these areas will ebb and flow depending on circumstances, and there are things you can do to protect yourself in each arena.

For example, when it comes to money and finances it is making sure that you have more than enough to cover your bills and have room to do and buy the things you'd like. The easiest way to do this is to have a portion of your income that you save and that you spend. Saving 20% - 10% that is locked away and 10% that is used to spend on more expensive items e.g. laptops, holidays etc., then portioning 55% toward bills, 5% for giving to others (charity etc.), 10% toward fun and 10% toward personal development or further training.

For health it is working out how much time you need to stay healthy and recharge. So for example, how much sleep is optimal for you? 8 hours is the recommended amount for adults, and studies show that not getting enough sleep is detrimental to mental as well as physical health. It is also thinking about how much exercise is optimal and what foods are best for you too.

In terms of mind it's important to work out what you need to feel mentally at peace. Maybe it's time with friends and a therapist, maybe its meditation, colouring in, art, music or time in the garden. How do you mentally turn off and let yourself recharge?

Success is a journey rather than a destination, the more that you can stay on the path and take in the scenery by looking after yourself, the more you can continue to grow and succeed.

Activity 17

Use a double page in your journal to come up with all of the different strategies you use to combat doubt. Give the page a grand title, like 'Doubt Busters', and give each a special bubble or style – this page is your turn-to reference for when you can feel doubt starting to creep in.

Finally, write a list of symptoms you would experience that indicate to you that you need to turn to one of these strategies.

Step 7 - Fulfilment

Lesson 1 - How To Recognise Fulfilment

When you are discontent, you always want more, more, more. Your desire can never be satisfied. But when you practice contentment, you can say to yourself, 'Oh yes - I already have everything that I really need'

Dalai Lama

Contentment is the feeling of satisfaction and happiness, whereas fulfilment is the satisfaction achieved from achieving something or reaching one's potential. In today's crazy and hectic world it can be hard to recognise either, there's always something else to do, or someone else to please. It's no wonder that people experience anhedonia, or the absence of pleasure in activities (men more than women).

There are several conditions which are often linked to introversion (but not necessarily related). Social anhedonia, which is separate from introversion, is characterised by a loss of interest in social activities and an increase in social withdrawal. Social anxiety on the other hand, another commonly linked condition, is typified by a loss of interest in social activities and an increase in anxiety symptoms. Introverts are typically more reserved and reflective, showing an interest in their own mental self, enjoying more solitary activities. When introverts choose friends, they do so wisely and their social circle shows much about who they trust. These various conditions will affect how the individual feels contentment.

It's likely that the activities that you do to gain contentment are going to be different from extroverts. Contentment is all about enjoying being lost in the moment, enjoying just being. Often you recognise it at the moment or with hindsight – it is very hard to plan to be contented!

Some people recognise contentment as that moment when they are so engrossed in the moment they are not worried or anxious about other things, others notice that they're not feeling stressed. These relate to an absence of negative symptoms.

During periods of contentment, some say they feel peaceful, rested or comfortable with themselves at that time. Your body feels at ease and your mind relaxed – these are positive signs of contentment.

Fulfilment is a step beyond contentment – it comes as a result of a journey or effect and is often related to a celebratory event (whether that is alone or with other people). Fulfilment by its very nature is more planned than contentment, you work towards achieving a milestone and when you get there you feel fulfilled and bask in the moment.

Being fulfilled does not mean that you are not still on a journey, we can be fulfilled and proud of our accomplishments so far, but recognise that our journey is not over. An example of this is that when going through this programme it's likely you will have several breakthrough moments. These can give an amazing sense of achievement and fulfilment, even though you are only part way through the programme, you don't stop, but you can enjoy the contentment that this discovery brings.

So far, this is all very straight forward, however that's until the brain comes in. Our brain is a marvellous thing, it helps us achieve all sorts of things, but it also holds us back. This is where the brain introduces the limiting beliefs that we spoke about in Step 3. Here's a few ways it might affect us:

Our physical ability – you can't skate, you can't swim that far, you aren't very good at running...

Our emotions – that always makes you feel sad, when someone does that it makes you angry, you don't need to sort this out – it's their fault...

Our mental capacity – you've never really understood maths, you're not very clever, you don't know how to do it – so give up...

Our social ability – no one likes you, they exclude you, they don't notice if you are there or not…

Our belief in ourselves – you never succeed, you always get things wrong, you'll end up regretting it…

Limiting beliefs are the voices that stop us applying for jobs, stop us from doing what we want with our lives, and stop us from taking the risks that help us to be successful. So it is important that people learn to keep their limiting beliefs in check.

Here's an easy one to challenge – do you remember as a child being told to clear your plate and not waste food? This comes from the time, only a couple of generations ago when food was rationed and families were only given a certain amount to live on. Therefore, no food could be wasted and even if you left something it was then used in something else the next day.

Now, if you sit down at a restaurant or for a meal cooked by someone else and your food is presented to you, they have chosen the portion size and how much you should expect to eat. A plateful is a meal in our subconscious mind. So to challenge that simple tricks like getting smaller plates will mean you eat less. If you are a person who forces yourself to clear the whole plate even when you are full, especially when it is something you love, then this is a subconscious belief that can be challenged in a different way.

Every meal, even more so when it's your favourite, challenge yourself to leave a mouthful on the plate and finish. Over time you will find that by doing this consistently, you break the belief that you must clear the plate and start to only eat what you want, rather than force yourself beyond that point.

You can challenge other self-limiting beliefs in similar ways – once you realise what the belief is, find a simple way of challenging it and showing it that it doesn't limit you. For example, if you have a self-limiting belief about speaking in public, try joining a book group, where members take it in turn to speak about a book they love – although this is public speaking, it will feel a lot more relaxed and less stressful, so you achieve a small goal and show that self-limiting belief that you can overcome it!

As you go through this journey to discovering the gift within you, you will be surprised about the number of self-limiting beliefs you come up against. Don't let them stress you, visualise them as naughty pixies trying to hold you back and find a way to outsmart them without them realising. Take the right approach and it can be fun!

Activity 18

In your journal spend 30 minutes writing or drawing what your ideal life would look like. Consider the following questions:

Where do you live?

Who do you live with (including pets)?

What is your home like? What can you see? What can you smell? What can you hear?

How do you make a living?

What friends are in your life (include ones you haven't met)?

What do you do with your spare time?

Lesson 2 - How To Achieve Fulfilment

If you love what you do, then you always find the time

Heidi Klum

There is more to life than just attaining your goals, especially if your goals are all about making the grade or getting the next promotion or more money.

While money and external success is useful, it doesn't necessarily lead to feeling fulfilled, doing work that you love to do and spending time with people you love can help you to achieve the fulfilment everyone desires. What this looks like in reality is different for each person and below are some ideas that may help you to live a life that leaves you feeling fulfilled.

Discover what you love to do by starting somewhere and see what you would rather be doing!

Mary Jane knew that she needed to shift her career after she developed Repetitive Strain Injury from her IT job and knew that she wanted to do something that helped people on a much deeper level than simply fixing their computers. Richard wanted to help people in his own way, rather than going round the hamster wheel again and again with a never ending work list.

Work is something that we spend the majority of our lives doing, so it's important to choose something that you have a passion in and interest for, because that will help to keep you going despite challenges. In the beginning you may just need to find a job to make money and when you realise that you'd rather be doing something else it's a good idea to take note of what that is and see how you can incorporate that into your days!

Following your dreams and seeking fulfilment isn't without its stresses, however stress in itself is not a bad thing, if you have a reason to endure it. In fact Viktor Frankl's book, Man's Search For Meaning shows that even the most harrowing of experiences can be endured if you have a strong enough reason! By making your work meaningful to you, your job can help you turn bad stress into good stress.

When he was employed, Richard had no control over his workload and could see that the impact of what he prided himself in was reducing as he became more overworked and stressed. For Mary Jane her IT work was stressful because she didn't really want to help people by fixing their machines, even though the work that the machines were doing helped people to develop our understanding of genetics and mental health. Being in business is also stressful but is easier to cope with because both of our businesses make a direct impact on the lives of our clients!

The reason you endure stress could be to get your work out into the world, as it was for Viktor Frankl, or it could be to make a difference to your family or the world at large. Maybe it is to solve a problem that has been restricting yourself or a loved one, and having these ties, these meaningful relationships will also help you in your quest for fulfilment.

So it's important to remember to take time for the relationships and people in your life while you are moving toward your goals.

These relationships can also support you to cope with the doubts as mentioned in the last lesson, especially if the people in your life are people who you trust. Doubts can be tricky and insidious thoughts and when you become aware of them, and learn to not believe them, you gain strength and trust in yourself, as well as other people.

When it comes to making sure you are living a fulfilled life it's important to have daily habits that support you to stay clear, calm and connected to your why.

Daily habits that you might want to try are meditation, Gratitude, affirmations, exercise or visualisation.

Meditation is something that is proven to relax and calm those who practice it regularly. It can be as simple as closing the door on distractions, sitting comfortably, closing your eyes and bringing your attention to your breathing. Counting each inhale and exhale up to 10 and then starting again at one for 5 minutes. It could be using a candle to keep your gaze on or focusing on how the air feels moving in and out of your nose and throat.

If the sitting still kind of meditation is difficult you could try a moving mediation like yoga or walking where you bring your focus to the poses or movement of your body.

Gratitude, either at the start or the end of the day, can really help you to bring to mind all the good things that you have experienced and encountered. It counters the brains natural tendency to focus on the negative, reduces stress and gives a more positive outlook on challenges we face. It also helps us to realise that we are a lot more abundant, able and successful than we thought, especially if we continue the practice over time.

Affirmations, are a great way to reprogram those negative beliefs that get in your way of achieving your goals and feeling fulfilled, whether your goal is to earn more money or to have healthy relationships, you can use these to help you stay focused on what you want to bring out to the world.

Exercise, apart from helping you to stay in peak physical condition to have the energy that you need, can also help you to achieve the mental clarity that is needed to succeed and feel fulfilled.

Visualisation is the process of relaxing your mind and picturing your desired outcome, how it feels, what it sounds like, how it smells. Whenever you find yourself struggling or facing a challenge, visualise your goal. This is a great way to stay focused on and reminded about why you are doing what you are doing and helps you to stay focused on bringing more of what you desire into the world.

As introverts it can be easy to get too far into our heads that we disconnect from the world and people around us. A daily habit that will prevent that from happening is to connect with the people we love. Whether that is through texts, emails, social media or grabbing a drink or a meal will help you to not only stay sane because you are forced to take a time out from your work, but also because it allows you to build healthy loving relationships with people that you can then share your success and happiness with.

Research has shown that the people who have the longest, healthiest and most fulfilled lives were those with more meaningful relationships. So while you are killing it with your goals and achievements, don't forget to nourish the important relationships in your life and you're on your way to getting, and staying fulfilled!

Activity 19

On a fresh page in your journal, write down the things that make you feel good in yourself.

Write down next to each one, how you feel after doing the activity.

Highlight the ones that you could do each morning or evening to put you in the right mindset for the day (or for sleep).

Write next to each one the amount of time you'd need for each.

Finally, write them in your diary (or on your calendar) in pen!

Endnote

There is no such thing as a pure introvert or extrovert. Such a person would be in the lunatic asylum

Carl Jung

Thank you for spending the time developing you!

Throughout this programme we have explained and shown you different areas related to your personality. We do so, not in an effort to change who you are, but more in a bid to help you to achieve the goals you want to achieve.

We've looked at goal setting, explored who you are, your support networks, how people see you, discussed other people in your world, how to develop at your peak performance and finally how to feel fulfilled.

Our aim is to help introverts move forward and identify how they can achieve the goals they set in Activity 1. Along the way there will be twists, turns and dead-ends, and the aim of the information we have shared in this programme is to enlighten the introvert into what to expect.

The people we help tell us that by following these seven steps, they can use the gift within them to achieve. They're the strategies that we have used in our lives to overcome the shackles holding us back and we know that they transform lives.

Here's to the first steps of your journey into the new you!

Activity 20

How do you now feel about the social problem you identified in Activity 1?

Write on a fresh page what the biggest social problem you now face is.

How do you feel about it?

About The Authors

Mary Jane Boholst was born and raised in south west London. She worked in IT before RSI made her rethink her career options and start her own business. As a formerly shy introvert she knows the challenges introverts face in today's extrovert world and is excited to share her strategies with you! She lives in London and enjoys challenging herself out of her comfort zone and hibernating when necessary!

Richard Daniel Curtis is an internationally recognised behaviour expert and multi-award winning business owner. His company The Mentoring School trains mentors around the world and his work with parents about children's behaviour has earned him the title The Kid Calmer. Richard has learned to deal with his introversion by being the gregarious host of social gatherings and events, often being mistaken for an extrovert. Nowadays he describes himself as more of an ambivert, using his introvert gifts to guide his social activities.